MW00795930

THE RAVEN
&
THE WOLF

Melissa Rodriguez

The Raven & The Wolf

© 2021, Melissa Rodriguez.

Print ISBN: 978-1-09837-7-618
eBook ISBN: 978-1-09837-7-625

THE RAVEN & THE WOLF

May the Wolf guide you along your path, and steer you away from danger. As it teaches you to trust your heart, and your soul through the many decisions you will face in your life.

As the Raven watches from above, and protects you from harm. Teaching you their wisdom, and intelligence from the life that they have seen from above.

May these two connect together to give you the strength, and wisdom to guide you through your life.

Dear Reader,

May the words that have been written within these pages speak to you in a way that you wish.

This book will be a path of happiness, sadness, love, and fiction. Welcome to my mind and thank you for joining me on this journey.

PERSONAL POEMS

Here are a collection of poems of the experiences I have been through. The feelings that I have kept locked down deep. It's time that I unlocked these doors that have kept these feelings at bay, and let the words write themselves to heal the pain from within.

The Writer

The mind of the spirit that flows through these words, that speaks what the mouth cannot.

Laying ink upon this paper as if the pen was taken from one's heart.

Writing its words that come from deep within, as if you are painting your soul with each stroke of your pen.

You fill these blank pages with every fiber of who you are, laying your life upon each page as you sacrifice your heart.

Eight was the age that everything changed for me.

You see that night is something I remember, and carry with me like an invisible backpack that no one can see. For that day was the day I saw the darkness in people.

For that was the day I saw everything get taken from us by a man I once called my stepdad.

You see at that young of an age I didn't quite understand what was happening, but as I grew older I understood what had happened.

The details of that day I overheard have registered in my brain and it hit me like a train.

To know while I was watching a Disney movie with my stepbrother that my mother was in the room behind me fighting for her life.

As my stepdad tied a rope around her neck trying to take the light from her eyes. I watched as the police did nothing, but stand by as he took everything.

From there it was like my mind turned off trying to shield me from the rest of that night.

For the next thing, I remembered was being in a truck with my mom and her friend on a road to Vegas.

But you see that day created a fracture within my soul that I never knew happened. A fracture that grew within years that now leaves my soul in shattered pieces.

I have seen so much over that time to know what that type of violence does to a person's soul that I would never what to damage the person I love, and put them through the exact same pain.

Silence

Be silent when he's on the phone.

Be silent when he's studying.

Be silent unless someone is talking to you.

Be silent to protect yourself.

Be silent when he's angry.

Do not speak, do not show emotion, tell white lies to keep yourself safe.

This is what I was taught at such a young age that it has made it difficult to use my voice as an adult. Which also made me scared to speak the truth in fear of what could happen.

Silence is what I have been taught and silence is what I need to break.

Wasted Time

Wasted Memories

Wasted Money

Wasted Feelings

Wasted these things just to have that moment of bliss that never lasted.

Lifeline

"Can you call my lifeline because I give up" How many of us have needed this type of call?

The call that wakes us up from that deep depression we feel on the inside.

The type of call that helps us take a step back from that ledge.

This type of call can come in many ways and is sometimes not from the people we hold close to us.

It can come from a song that we connect with, from a quote or poem that we have read, from a show that we are watching, and even from a podcast that we are listening to.

For myself I know I have needed this type of call many times before and have received it in various ways.

Each time this call brought life back into my soul and shattered the doubt that fueled my depression.

Once that doubt was shattered I realized that I can overcome anything depression brings onto the battlefield.

As I stand here frozen in fear watching as it gracefully walks by as if its floating across this wooden floor.

I watch as you turn your head and we lock eyes right before you fade away into the other room.

Those eyes that have stuck with me for years to come as they were a scarlet red.

I can see that you are trying to figure me out, watching my every move to see if you can read me like a book, but these pages are closed and locked down tight.

As we make eye contact I can see that you are searching to see if my eyes will be a gateway to who I really am.

Don't they say that a person's eyes are the windows to their soul, but when you look into my eyes can you see my demons swimming around in my darkness.

Can you see the battle that wages on in my mind and soul. You will never be able to see that because I will only show you the pages that I want you to see.

You trying to figure me out is like trying to open Pandora's box.

Once you open it, it can never be closed

and you will be surrounded by the demons that have plagued my mind since the beginning of time that has been locked away for quite some time.

Roots are what connect you to your culture.

Roots are what connect you to your ancestors.

Roots make up the very essence of who you are.

But what do you do when you have never been taught about your roots?

Feeling as if you don't belong in either world.

Feeling as if you can't connect to others who are the same as you.

Being disregarded because one of your parents had decided not to teach you their language.

Being left in the dark feeling as if you may never belong.

Roots that have never been connected, but have been severed.

Fighting on your own to figure out what these roots are and what they could have been if they were just connected at a young age.

LOVE

Is such a powerful word that we use on a daily basis

You say it to your mother, father, and siblings.

You say it to your sons and daughters.

You say it to your closest friends.

And most of all you say it to your wives, husbands, girlfriends, and boyfriends.

The first three are the ways that I use the word love, and the last one is a feeling that is foreign to me.

You see I've never really seen that type of love or have been around it.

I have seen false love and damaging love.

A love that was never true and a love that left you broken.

I have seen love being mistaken for lust.

Love that left you with bruises, and a love so strong that it left you crippled, to think that you can't live without it.

Being around these types of love since a young age has left me terrified to ever truly be in love. That once I get close to it, I turn and run as fast as I can.

For you see I have fallen victim to those types of love and have seen those close to me fall victim as well.

So, my love is protected by a thick wall that even a bullet couldn't penetrate it.

Because I fear that if I truly let you in and fall in love with you that one-day ill fall victim again to the lies that come with that four letter word LOVE.

Depression calls out to me like an old friend I haven't seen in ages.

As if it left to live in a different country for the time being until it decides to return. Being mentally picked up from the airport and brought back to its old home. Calling me to let me know how much it has missed me and how it can't wait to see me again.

I mentally open the door and hug depression as we go to sit down to talk about everything that has happened.

I listen as depression goes on and on about everything I have been through. Making me over think on things I wish I could erase.

Once depression stops talking it gets up and says goodbye as it walks out the door, leaving me numb with my thoughts.

Back to the days

I wish I could go back to the days when I was fearless.

Back to the days when my smile was real.

Back to the days when I was more adventurous.

Back to the days when I would be able to open up.

Back to the good times of my childhood.

Back to the days before my depression and anxiety showed up.
Before everything that screwed me up mentally.

Wish I could just go back to the days where I was free to be me,
without questioning myself.

Darkness is like a friend. It meets up with you every once in a while to catch up. It comes and goes as it pleases. Sometimes you grow apart and sometimes it's there for the long run. Darkness is the friend you cry with and share all of your hidden emotions with that nobody else knows about. It can also turn on you and make you feel like you're nothing in this world.

Light is like a lover. It is there every day of every minute. It wakes up beside you and greets you with a soft touch upon your skin. It smiles at you every day and lets you know everything will be okay. Even when darkness shows up to meet, the light still sits by your side throughout the night until darkness leaves. It lies next to you each night at the end of the day to wake up to you the next morning to spend its day with you yet again.

So, you see throughout your life you will have your moments with the darkness, but the light will be with you for eternity.

Getting to taste that life again made me realize that I craved that type of love.

Someone who I could love and would love me with no expectations.

Jumping from one to another made me realize that I am afraid to be alone.

Making the same mistakes that I have seen as a child.

Having that feeling of not wanting to grow old regretting not really being in love.

Regretting not sharing those moments with someone who truly makes me happy.

Someone who makes me smile just by thinking of their name.

I need to bring in this fear of being alone and remind myself that it's okay to be alone. That it will take time to find the person who will truly make me happy.

Vulnerability

Once you show vulnerability it's like people around you can smell it and attack like vultures ripping you apart piece by piece.

For they love the smell and how each piece they tear apart is a piece that makes them feel whole again in the existence of their hollow shells that hold their fractured selves.

For they do not know that we can see their vulnerability within their eyes, but we do not attack like vultures.

Instead, we come to them in a sign of a dove to spread the love that was given to us to show them the path to righteousness.

To help them achieve self-love for themselves to brighten that hollow shell to make it feel whole once again.

This life that I have seen
terrifies me to the depths of my soul.

That I run and continue to run
till I can no longer feel this feeling.

This feeling of love that you have shown me that I have never known
is so foreign to me that I shut down, and my first instinct is to push
you so far away from me that you leave.

I know that I would only destroy you and the thought of love that
you have seen.

The type of love that I cannot give you,
for you see I'm a damaged soul trapped in ways that you have
never seen.

Ways that I fear would only drive you away if you really knew, so
yes I am terrified of the love you can bring.

So please I beg you if I start to push you away bring me in closer
and don't let go like the others.

For I know I can love you same if you only show me how.

Anxiety.

I like to come out when she walks into a crowded room. Making her feel as if everything is ten times louder, and feel as if she is out of place. What I do is make her dislike going to places in fear that she is being judged.

Depression.

I like to come out to make her feel like she's not enough. Make her feel as if she is failing in her life and feel as if it will never get better. I bring up everything that is dwelling within her to the point she breaks.

When we decided to mix together and hit her with full force, it will make her feel as if the walls around her are closing in and her emotions go numb.

Who am I?

Am I the product of a childhood full of despair and pain?

Or

Am I a product of a childhood that left me with armor so strong that I can handle what this world brings to me?

Who am I?

Am I a person trapped by anxiety and depression?

Or

Am I a warrior who conquers these enemies and makes it through?

Who am I?

Am I a person who stays a victim?

Or

Am I a person who can push through and become a survivor?

Who am I?

Am I a product of domestic violence?

Or

Am I a product of a strong-willed person who knows when to walk away?

These are just some of the circumstances that we go through in our lives.

You can either let these circumstances hinder you from achieving greatness or you can use them to learn and grow from.

This life will throw many different types of obstacles in your way, but it's how you come out the other side that will build your strength.

Can't you see that I'm falling?

That I'm screaming out for help.

Why can't you see that my life is collapsing?

Why can't you see that I hide behind a mask and a smile, so you won't ask me questions but why can't you see that it never reaches my eyes.

Do you even notice that I'm depressed? Would you even care if you did?

Answer this question would you regret not being there if l died tomorrow?

How loud do I have to scream out for you to finally see that I need help?

Do I need to scream at the top of lungs for you to finally notice.

I'm running through this dark forest passing these trees at a speed no human can reach. Jumping over fallen trees to get away from what is chasing me.

I run and continue to run until I finally reached the end and let me tell you it's certainly site to see.

I stand here watching as the sun rises shining its beautiful glow across the sky and the water below.

I turn to look behind me at the dark forest that I just ran through and see how the brightness of the sun chases away the darkness that once filled this forest, showing me a side that I did not see.

This forest that was once so dark is now beautiful, bright, and filled with life. Letting me know that whatever darkness I go through there is always a light that will shine through and show me the way out.

A light that will always be there and in the end will show me the beauty that I went through.

This life is like holding sand within my hands.

Watching as each grain slip between the cracks, as I desperately try to tighten my grip.

No matter how tight I make it, they always seem to slip away.

Leaving just one small grain of sand to light the hope within that one day I will find this grain of sand that will turn my world right side up again.

Negative Mind

One pill

Two pill

Three pill

Fuck it, just take a handful.

Erase this pain you feel on the inside.

Erase the memories that broke you.

Erase the people who made you feel like shit.

Just erase the life from within you.

Tell me can you feel it.

Can you feel the blood flowing through your veins?

Can you feel yourself growing colder?

Can you feel yourself getting tired?

Just sleep and everything will be alright.

Positive Mind

NO! don't do it

Drop those pills from your hand.

Don't listen to that negative mind.

The pain you feel on the inside shows that you have emotions.

Those memories that haunt you make you into the strong and powerful person you are today.

The people that made you feel like shit showed you that snakes live in this world.

Don't ever erase the life from within you, because you are meant to be here.

Tell me can you feel that.

Can you feel the fire within you growing?

Can you feel yourself getting stronger?

Can you feel yourself gaining more energy?

Forget sleeping, get out there and chase your dreams.

Origami

I sit and I watch as you take this blank slate and delicately fold lines within it to create such different shapes.

I watch in such wonderment as you transform this blank slate into such art.

With each intricate fold that you have created you have turned this blank slate into what you wished for it to be.

Not knowing that this blank slate you were folding was me.

The raindrops hit my windshield and dash away like shooting stars.

Takes me back to the time when I was younger with nothing to worry about.

While I sat in that truck with it being pitch black outside. I felt as if I was in a spaceship dashing through the stars on some expedition through the universe.

This is one of the amazing memories I have as a child.

Not being able to sleep due to these thoughts racing around in my mind. As my body feels energized, but my mind feels heavy with such pain.

Hearing this light knocking in the back that I have been trying to silence, but it just keeps getting louder and louder by the minute. I'm sorry depression, but I can't handle you right now.

Reminding myself over and over again that everything is okay in this moment, and that we are on a different path then what we used to be on.

As I repeat this in my mind the knocking starts to fade lower and lower until it can no longer be heard. My mind starts to regain its peace and comes back from that moment of disruption.

When I was younger I always had this recurring dream that still to this day I don't know what it means.

This dream was always the same and never changed. I would fall asleep and wake up in this huge white room as if it was never-ending.

In this room, it would just be me and when I looked around I would see this person in the distance. I would always call out to this person saying hello and they would turn to look at me.

Then in a blink of an eye, he would be in front of my face bent over since he was so tall.

He would be wearing this black suit with a white shirt and a black tie, which never changed. But his face is what scared me the most. It was as white as a sheet of paper with no hair. There were no eyes, no mouth, and no nose. All that his face showed was like a white noise screen moving at the speed of lightning.

This would frighten me to the point of waking up instantly. I have had this dream many times as a child, but once I grew older this dream never came again.

As we print these pages of our lives, hoping that each mark of the ink takes away the pain from inside.

We print these pages in hope to heal not only ourselves but those who feel what we feel.

For each page filled is like a transfer of ink from our souls to this paper as we heal.

My body goes numb as a switch goes off in my head.

It's as if I feel nothing at all,

My thoughts die down as everything around me goes silent.

But this is when my demons speak their mind,
as I reach for this blade and lay it upon my skin.

This delicate dance begins,
as it glides across its canvas.

A dance so gentle that it doesn't bring attention.

For this dance is what brings me back and once it's done,
my body comes back from being numb.

This dance has been my escape many times,
but once I got older this dance changed.

My demons grew stronger when I lived
one of the worst times in my life.

They became more vocal in dark, as if they
would sit right next to me while I lay in bed.

As they would tell me lies,

but at the time I believed them.

This dance took a turn as I took a

handful of painkillers to make it all stop.

As I lay back in my bed, I can feel the

blood as it travels in my veins.

As I fall asleep to the quietness of the night,

thinking that maybe this was the end.

But I woke up the next day and put on my mask,

so no one would see my pain.

Days have passed as my demons have been silent,

as if they were creating a plan waiting to attack.

As I was at my lowest point being kicked while I was down.

They decided to show with vengeance
telling me lies that I couldn't handle at the time.

I grabbed a knife and held it to my throat as tears escaped from my
eyes, as all I could hear is their words to end it all once and for all.

But I couldn't, so I fall to my knees as I dropped the knife begging
for them to stop as I continued to cry.

With no one there to turn to I went back into my room,
as I cried until I fell asleep.

When my eyes reopened it was no longer dark in this gloomy room,
but bright as the sun came through.

Right then and there I remembered what happened last night
as I turned to my faith and begged for strength.

From that point on I decided that enough was enough and
I was no longer going to let what other people say affect me.

For I know who I am, and since that day my strength has never
failed me.

I have locked my demons away so tight for they can never escape.

For if I ever start to feel down, my dance turned to music,

reading or writing to help take me away for that moment until my mind is relaxed.

Because I vowed to never return to that dance for I am better than that.

I'm locked in a cage with bars so close that I can't escape.

With the person who I once was being ripped away from me leaving my soul in two.

All I can do is look upon that person and cry out to them to try and return to me.

But that person cannot hear me for their path to me is blocked by my doubt, depression, and anxiety.

Doubt stole my carefree soul once I started being scared of people's opinions of me.

Depression stole my carefree soul once I started to understand things fully.

Anxiety stole my carefree soul by putting these little negative thoughts in my mind.

You see these are three of the major battles I go through to reunite my souls back together each and every day.

Sometimes I am victorious in these battles and sometimes I fall victim as well in these battles.

I don't see what you see.

I don't see the beautiful person you see when you look at me. No, I see this broken glass with these faint cracks and deep cracks to shattered pieces.

So how can you say beautiful? You must not really know me or have been close enough to see my soul.

You see my soul. My Soul!

Is a dark place filled with empty grounds that never end. You see my soul has been torn, written on, stepped on, and stained on by the words of my past.

You see my past is not squeaky clean. For most people they probably thought my life was amazing.

To see the things I received but they didn't see the strings attached to these things.

You see for every tattoo that lies on my skin is like a patch that replaces the torn skin of my past. For these tattoos bring me closer to the me that I see for they hold a story.

For my story is deep and thoughts go deeper for if you stay and weather the storm that comes with each page you might just reach the end of this story.

Brick by Brick

Brick by brick as I build this wall.

Brick by brick as I silence your voice.

Brick by brick to keep these fights silent.

Brick by brick to close out these harmful memories.

Brick by brick to forget your touch.

Brick by brick to close off these emotions.

Laying each brick down to create a new layer. As I reach for my ladder to build it higher.

Once I lay down this last brick, I climb down from this ladder and take a step back.

I look up at this wall that I have built over the years to keep these words and emotions out.

But you know what's funny is that the words you have spoken to me, the abuse that I have seen, the fights that I have overheard, the doubts, and worthlessness that I have felt have stained these walls in permanent ink.

I remember when I met you in 8th grade. We started out as friends and as time moved on we became so much more than that.

Our relationship was fun all the way until sophomore year of high school. That's when everything changed. You became more posses- sive, forceful, and mentally abusive.

You would tell me all the time that I need to lose weight even though I was only 125. Those words mentally stuck with me still to this day that whenever I go over that weight I feel disgusted with how I look and feel as if nobody will find me attractive.

Then that time during soccer practice where I asked you to leave because I would get in trouble with my coach and you wouldn't until I kissed you. I remember you trapping me in between the gate and you, so I wouldn't have a way out. I asked you to leave multiple times, and then you grabbed my jaw forcing me to look at you and proceeded to aggressively kiss me.

The final straw for me was when we were hanging out after school just us and you thought it would be funny to push me up against the tennis court gates and press a pocket knife up to my throat. You looked me dead in the eyes and I would not show you any type of fear. You could have easily moved that blade across my throat and ended my life.

I went home that day and I couldn't do it anymore. I couldn't be in this toxic relationship, so I broke up with you through a text because I didn't have the guts to do it in person and I remember you telling that the next time you saw me you were going to lay your hands on me.

I was so terrified to run into you at school, but then I received news from our mutual friends that you moved to a different school. I felt such a relief that day, but I thank you for showing me that I never want to date someone like that ever again.

I witness your hands wrapped around her neck like a snake. Watching terrified as her face turns red.

I scream for you to stop and as you turn your face I no longer see the person I knew, but a man filled with rage.

You run towards me in attempt to slap the phone out of my hand as I feel your fingertips graze my face.

Stuck in shock as you grab my wrists with such force I never knew. Screaming out for ones help to notice she's no longer in the room.

Once freed I run to my room and brace myself between the door and the dresser praying to let me be strong enough to hold this door closed.

I sat there terrified of what was going to happen next, thinking about nothing but the worse. I knew I had to get out of this home, but I was so scared to open the door.

When I had the courage to get out I opened the door and ran across the hall to my closest exit.

Opening the door that lead to the garage, I hit the button until it opened just enough that I knew I could run and make it under not leaving a chance of getting caught.

I ran as fast as I could diving under the garage door as the ground scraped my knees. Finally free from that home I ran down the street, until I heard someone calling out my name.

Running into the arms that raised me at our neighbors home as we sat with them waiting for the cops to arrive.

I wish that I could go back to where nightmares were just that of a dream, but some nightmares spill over into reality.

I lay in this dark room being half asleep when you came in. I felt the blankets move as you slide under and came closer to me. I remember freezing up when you pushed my front up against the wall. Being twice my size I couldn't move, fuck I was scared to move.

I felt your hands as you moved them across my body under my clothes grabbing and touching what you pleased. I felt so disgusted with myself thinking this was my fault. Maybe I gave you signals that this was what I wanted.

Then the door opened as someone looked in, you didn't stop running your hands on my skin and I silently prayed that they would say something, but a word never left their mouth as they just closed the door and left.

You kept going with touching me in place I didn't want you to touch. You must have gotten bored with me not reciprocating your advance, because you pulled back and left this room leaving me with this disgusted feeling.

I wanted to cry once you left, shit I wanted to take a shower and scrub my body raw to get rid of your touches. As I grew older I understood that it wasn't my fault, that I didn't deserve what you did. I did nothing wrong, but you did.

You damaged a part of me that night. A part of me that I am still struggling to piece back together.

I bundle up my past wrapping it in a black string holding together all of my pain, anxiety, and depression that I have felt through the years.

Walking in the darkness of my mind to a space where I can lay this bundle upon the floor covering it inch by inch with lighter fluid.

Lighting these matches causing a glow in this dark place as I take a breath releasing my grip watching them slowly fall making contact with my past as it goes up in flames, burning so bright this darkness is pushed back from every corner of the room.

This bundle turning into nothing but ashes as the fire dies down. Sitting here watching as a new light starts to emerge as it grows stronger and stronger by the minute.

Creating a new feeling, a new breath, and a new life to this once dark room as I pull off this mask throwing it into the trash as it is no longer needed.

Learning that my life is no longer suppressed by my past, but is now free from the cage it once called home like a phoenix being reborn from the ashes of its past life.

These thoughts and memories breaking free of their suppression sending my mind into a mental disarray.

This chaos that has overtaken has sent me on an emotional roller-coaster that has turned my heart heavy.

These emotions that have made it hard to breathe while making it harder to keep those tears at bay.

I've been hiding behind this disguise for so long that all these thoughts, memories, and emotions are starting to create cracks as I rush to grab this tape before anyone notices.

How can I be me, when I don't even know who I am completely?

Ripped in three of the different sides of me. One who is shy and quiet, one who wishes to be free, and one who is a mystery.

Every part of me I wish to bring whole, but how can that be when each side is terrified of what the world will think.

Being what others wish of me has destroyed the person I have inside of me.

Starting from the beginning searching for these three in hopes that one day I will be set free.

Used to the Darkness

I've laid next to these monsters for so long that I no longer know how to sleep without them. They have attached themselves to me like a second skin, so they can never be forgotten.

Sitting with me every day as they look upon this world through my eyes while they sit in the darkest parts of my mind.

As they drive people away that get to close fearing that they would help me loosen the chains that bind me to them.

One comes out as it wraps their hands around my mouth to keep me quiet, when I have something to say. Whispering that what I might say is never needed.

One sticks around and stirs the pot while it waits for the perfect time to explode like a bull running out of its cage.

One decides to make an appearance when they feel like making me depressed. Walking around my home not wanting to do anything like eeyore.

The last one has been with me the longest. They come out when they feel like turning off my emotions, so that I feel nothing. As if they turn on the switch that makes me go numb and unbothered.

These monsters have been with me for as long as I can remember. Some have been here the longest, while the others showed up throughout the years.

Why can't you open up?

Have you seen what they do to those who open up? They take advantage of your words and twist them later on to just hurt you.

How do you know it will happen with them?

I don't but I still can't do it. I can't trust people that easily with what I have been through.

You can't take that with you and believe that these people are the same.

That's easy for you to say, but you should know since you were there as well.

I know I was but I can't take that baggage with me for eternity.

I know we can't but how can you just drop that off and move forward?

Because I know that if I bring it with me I will never be able to live my life fully.

I don't know if I can fully let go and heal like you can.

I understand, but I know deep down that you can.

How do you know that I can?

Because I am you and you are me.

Sitting in this dark room with nothing, but music playing as my emotions overwhelm my body.

Feeling everything at once from sadness to anger to depression to feeling numb.

As old habits start calling my name like sirens tempting me to return to them.

Hearing their sweet music as it pulls on my strings pulling me closer and closer to where I'm just in arms reach.

While they reach out to me their music starts to falter as I awaken in that split second and pull away from them.

Turning my back as I walk away I can hear them calling for me to come back as I continue to walk away their voices start to fade away.

You terrify me

I feel as if you can read me like a book that is closed tightly, and that terrifies me.

As if you will be that one person who will sneak in without being seen, and that terrifies me.

When you look at me it feels like you are seeing right through me reading the pages that are inside my soul, and that terrifies me.

It's like you are able to take apart the way I think and process it in ways nobody can, and that terrifies me.

I'm like a scattered puzzle that with every answer I give, you figure out what pieces connect together to help paint a clearer picture, and that terrifies me

But as much as it terrifies me it also intrigues me because I want to know what you can read, and what chapter you get to.

The river flows with such calmness and peace as if it has never known anything different. If you follow its path you will find that this once calm river turns ferocious with such power and strength tearing through the rocks in its path.

This river that would rip your feet off the ground if you dare enter its waters, but if you continue to follow its path at a safe distance you will see that this river turns back to its peaceful ways opening up to a site so breath taking and beautiful.

My life is that of this river. Starting out so peaceful, and then turning into something so ferocious that tore me from my core. Shattering every inch of who I was while staining my soul with such darkness.

Then I realized who I wanted to be and turned this darkness back to its peaceful ways as my healing, and mending of myself turned into such beauty.

Deep down her soul is both chaotic and peaceful.

Your hands glide across my skin bringing me into a warm embrace washing away the memories of my past.

As you lay your lips lightly on my skin as you kiss softly up my neck cleansing away the pain I feel within.

As your eyes lock onto mine with a love I have never known. We start to lean into each other like two magnets that can never be apart.

Our lips lock with a strong passion that I knew from that moment on I am all yours.

I need to release and unscrew this mind that is so wound tight that any minute it will explode.

Drawers being filled to the brim and filing cabinets so full that nothing new can fit in.

Trying to shove so much in that processing takes a minute.

Overworking my mind and sending it into overtime.

Trying to send papers to the shredder that is no longer in need and saving those that I will forever need.

Needing my medicine to cope with all this information flowing through this mind.

With this dim light and music playing this screw seems to unwind.

With every hit of this beat sending a wave of tranquility my mind finally feels at peace.

Sometimes master pieces are made from

broken pieces piled together like a puzzle piece.

Taking the pieces from the many different broken puzzles that lay
within, gluing them together and

taping them down to create new pieces.

The pieces that have come from my anxiety, depression,

self-doubt, happiness, pain, and experience sure have created such
a beautiful master piece.

To the future me,

So many years have passed and so many things to look forward to. To the future me don't stress because whatever you are going through will pass. You will become the person you were always meant to be. You will meet people who will leave and those who were destined to stay. You will grow from each and every day that goes by. You will move closer to your dreams and closer to the one you are meant to meet. Just learn from the mistakes you will make and be stronger every day. Don't stress so much on what others think and stay true to yourself and your beliefs.

To the future me, I wish you nothing but the best and I can't wait to meet you one day.

FICTION
& QUOTES

Here are a collection of poems that have come to my mind from many different inspirations that I have come across. Now these poems are that of imagination and small quotes that I have written down.

Your beauty shines brighter than the moon itself.

Capturing me within this moment as I can hear my heart start pounding.

Falling faster and faster every minute my eyes are locked upon yours.

Feeling this warmth as it covers my body like a warm blanket on a winter night.

Knowing that this was the moment I finally knew what true love feels like.

Even in the darkest of your days. If you look within, you will find the light to lead your way.

Welcome to the City of the Lost.

Where you will find many who are lost in different ways.

Yes, I do see that this place is dark and cold, but what do you expect when you're lost.

Some of us have been here for years, months, and some of us are brand new.

We go through this vast dark lonely place searching for our way back to our path.

If you are new to this place this search will be blinding and feel hopeless, but if you keep searching your eyes will adapt to the dark and you will slowly be able to see.

The search back to your light will be a journey with many cracks in the road that will try to trick you into staying in the City of the Lost.

So, beware of your steps and keep up your armor because, in the end, you will make it out of the City of the Lost.

When I say "I love you to the moon and back", I meant it with everything in me.

When I say "I love you to the moon and back", it means I love you for all your faults.

When I say "I love you to the moon and back", it means I love you for all your mood swings.

When I say "I love you to the moon and back", it means I love you for your independent ways.

When I say "I love you to the moon and back", it means I love you on the days you don't love yourself.

When I say "I love you to the moon and back", it means I love you for the days you feel insecure.

When I say "I love you to the moon and back", it means I love you for every good day to every bad day.

So, when I say "I love you to the moon and back", I genuinely mean it with every beat of my heart.

Don't let the judgment of others hold you down.

There is only one person who can judge you and he looks deep within your heart and soul. Even with what is shown he will love you regardless.

As time flies by and starts to fade will you be the one who rides time like a wave or will you take advantage of what time creates.

With every movement within the clock is a shot to take will you take that shot or will you watch it fade?

From every minute to the hour is a time of change. Will you make that change or stay the same.

In the end, it's up to you to use time as you wish.

So I ask you this, will you stand by as time passes you by or will you use your limited time before it escapes?

Tick tock goes the clock said the grand master of time.

For you cannot stop until the clock reaches the top.

At the top, there is a spot you see for at this spot lies a way for you to see that of what the clock hides so deep.

The grand master of time wraps his arm around me as he says "Don't you see the beauty that lies so deep from within this time, you can see everything that lies within your eyes"

I look down from this spot with such wonder and amazement of what hides so deep within this time being shown to me.

The beauty that this clock holds is that of true wonder as the colors fade between the ticks and the tocks of this clock.

We stay in this spot and watch as time ticks and tocks away turning day to night.

As time reaches the top we climb down from
this spot as I thank the grand master of time for the wonder he has shown me that this clock hides.

Forbidden Love

We loved with a love that was irreplaceable even though our love was forbidden.

For we only saw each other and what our souls could be for no one could keep us apart.

For our love was stronger than that of the word itself.

For our souls have connected and intertwined that our love would never fail.

For you see she is my world and I would give up my life for our love.

I will fight till the end of time
to see our love be set free and to show my love for the world to see.

What you see is different from what I see.

For you see we capture this beauty differently.

For you capture this beauty in a different light. For as I capture it with a different sight.

The beauty that we see in which we hold with such wonder is that of a similar sight being held in a different light.

Life is a growing process that you
make from the mistakes you have made.

In a world full of chaos and hate

We strive to find those who are not afraid to blur the lines of different cultures, who see people for their personalities and not by the color of their skin.

Who join together to fight those who threaten to take our rights away like rebels taking on a king.

American Dreams

We start this life being taught about the American dream. Throughout the years this dream has been dying out and replaced with greed.

This right that was given since the beginning is no longer given to those who have a different culture, race, religion, sexual orientation, and skin color.

This right that is being taken away by greedy politicians who only want what's best for themselves and not for everyone in this country.

We stand more divided by the system that has been put in place to protect us that has now turned against us.

We walk these streets in protest to show that we are united as one against this system.

We peacefully protest to write these wrongs that have been done upon our brothers and sisters.

We fight for a change in a system that only sees us by the color of our skin and not by who we really are as individuals.

We link arms with those of different races and cultures to show that your fight is not just yours but is ours.

We stand in the face of this system as we demand this change to happen to treat us as equals no matter the skin color or the title we hold.

We are all human beings no matter the culture or the color of our skin.

We are alike and we should fill this world with love and not with hate.

"To be or not to be"

What an excellent question. A question so deep with such few words that make you think.

A process where we as humans try to figure out who we are, but sadly for most of us, we leave that decision to those we surround ourselves with, to be forever molded by others until the day we break away.

These people who mold us could also be the closest to us, who affect our lives throughout our time on this earth.

To be successful or to not be successful

To be an athlete or to not be an athlete

To be the golden child or to not be the golden child

To be compliant or to not be compliant

To be ourselves or to not be ourselves

With so many questions on who we can or cannot be that is laid upon our shoulders weighing us down like an anchor attached to our feet as we sink into the words of how others want us to be.

I say we break free from that anchor that holds us down and become who we see deep down inside us.

Speak with love and not with hate.

Spread the light and not the darkness.

Live with peace and not with chaos.

Lead with courage and not with fear.

Most of all be yourself and not what others want you to be.

From the brightest days to the darkest nights.

As you awaken to see another day in a city full of life.

You face the mirror to see the inner demons that plague your life with a never-ending battle.

As you fight to keep them away from the inner light that is left within you.

When you head out to face the day you fear that your light will succumb to the darkness throughout the day.

As the battle wages on between your inner light and the demons that plague your mind till day falls to night.

As you lay down to rest for the night you smile knowing that your inner light has won the battle once again.

They say the eyes are the windows to your soul.

When you look into mine can you see the answers you are searching for or do you get lost in the deep storm of what my soul is?

Forever Forgotten

Forever forgotten as they locked me in this cage.

Forever forgotten from the minds of those I influenced.

Forever forgotten from the minds of those I once loved.

Forever forgotten by the society I once cared for.

They left me to be forever forgotten for they thought I was crazy for the ways that I think.

They prosecuted me because I frightened their reality as I tried to bring light to the unjust ways of our society.

They took me at night without making a sound, as if I just left within the night.

Nothing moved from its place as if my home was a museum collecting dust as I will be forever forgotten.

Freedom is not being trapped by everyday life.

Isn't it strange how the mind works?

How we have these little wire highways that send these little balls of light to each section to each side.

That somehow reminds us to breathe, to think, to remember, to see, to feel pain, to feel our heartbeat.

How strange it can be that sometimes our minds hold back memories that could harm us mentally to help protect our sanity.

But it's strange to me how some of us can destroy the one thing that helps us through the day.

How we neglect our minds from improving and learning by not simply reading a book or even playing a game that engages our minds.

Our brains are an instrument of knowledge that once you poison it, it dies slowly and starts to lose its knowledge.

If people saw me talking to myself would they think I'm psychotic and toss me away to an institution just to be thrown into a straitjacket into a padded room to be forgotten about as if I never existed.

But don't they say the ones who talk with themselves are the most intelligent. Is that why I'm in this white room because they are frightened by my presence.

Is it because I see this world for what it is when they still see this allusion that they don't want to be lifted.

As I sit in this white room as they try to destroy my resistance to convert me to see this allusion to blind me from what's happening behind the curtain.

As I announce that they will never break my resistance or my ability to defy what they want me to become which is a mindless human being clueless and unaware of my surroundings, blending into the backgrounds they want to create for me.

Another puppet hanging lifeless from their strings.

As this man lies down to sleep he fears his dreams for you see he believes he is slowly being driven mad by what he sees.

For this dream comes back to him each night as he slumbers.
For this dream is that of a woman he sees but can never reach as all he hears are her distant screams.

For you see, she is a distant memory of man haunted by his past of a woman long forgotten by society.

For she was taken by a man that no one has seen for he walks in the shadows of the night like a reaper waiting for his next victim to fright.

This man turned his back in fear for what he might have seen if he turned to face the window that leads to see the reaper who hunts at night for women to steal.

For this night will forever be burned into his mind of the screams that will haunt him till the end of time.

As the darkness of the night falls in this town and as the moon shines through his room as he sits on a chair in the comer hearing the distant screams of a woman crying out for help.

He pleads and begs for her to stop to take away the guilt that he feels, as he falls to his knees crying out for her to stop but you see she cannot rid him of his guilt for he is the keeper of that guilt for she is just that of a distant memory.

As I lay here in this grave that has been left without a name but just a number.

For myself, I am number 66 for there are others just like me and many more that will meet the same end as I.

As I walk around the place that I took my last breathe I wonder if those who put me in this place every think about me or even if they visit me but how could they when I'm just number lost in a sea of graves.

For my life will be forgotten as time passes and the place that I took my last breath has met its demise by those who have called it immoral, unfair, and just plain evil for what the doctors have put us through.

For myself, I'm stuck here to roam around this place with others just like me who have lost their name as I have.

As I walk these halls and sea of graves I wonder if my name will ever be given back to me and if those who have forgotten me if maybe just one day they will wonder what has become of me, but until then I am lost to the sea of graves only known by my number 66.

As I sit in this dark room with the glow of this dim light I can feel them surrounding me as I feel their breath upon my skin as goose-bumps arise.

I feel a cold shiver runs through my veins. As they whisper nothing but sweet sins they wish for me to commit.

I can feel their cold touch as they lay their hands upon my skin as I sit frozen to this world.

I hear nothing but their voices so dark and menacing as they persuade me to join them.

As my vision grows cloudy I can feel myself slipping into this dark world as I feel their energy running through my body as they show me the dreams I can achieve with their help.

As I feel their lips upon my ears as they whisper so sweetly "All this can be yours with a little price of a simple sacrifice"

With my vision returning as I start to become free

I hear one last thing like a whisper in the wind "three days and we will return"

Deceitful One

We know him by many names,

but one name stands out from the rest "Lucifer".

He comes to us in many shapes and forms, but in the end, only wants us for one thing.

He will deceive us to no end to get what he wants and desires.

He will send his demons to try and break us.

He will show no mercy as he drags us down into the darkness to this bottomless hell.

Forever to hold us captive in our addiction, that lead us into this place.

But do not show fear for there is a way to escape his enchantment.

For you are far stronger than he is and have a stronger army to defeat his pawns.

So pour your belief into God and he will set you free.

I walk this earth oh so numb. This heart of mine you see, it does not work, for it does not beat.

The blood that flows through my veins is nothing but a cold chill that leaves me frozen. I walk around so lost and emotionless seeing nothing but hate around me.

As I walk through these gloomy streets contemplating these wicked thoughts, as I look up to meet your eyes that hold a sense of warmth and kindness, I'm taken back by such a beautiful sight.

You smile my way and I swear I felt my heartbeat for the first time in years. As you walk my way I feel my body heat up as I get nervous not knowing what this new feeling is.

As you introduce yourself with a voice that should belong to the heavens, as you radiate this warmth that I have not known in years.

Within our conversation, I ask myself, why this intelligent beautiful soul is speaking to someone so cold. Being lost in my thoughts, you ask me if I would like to grab a coffee with you, and how could I decline as you look at me with this spark in your eyes.

As you grab my hand to lead the way, I feel this electricity run through my veins sending my nerves into shock.

As we sit at this little cafe at a table in the comer with a cup of coffee in between my hands as I listen to you talk; with the warmth of this coffee, I contemplate how

it doesn't give me that same warmth as you give me.

The time flies by as you look at your phone and realize how late it had gotten. I walk you to your car as we exchange numbers, as you tell me to keep in touch.

As I watch you drive away, I can feel the

warmth that you have given me fade away as your car fades from sight.

As we meet up for weeks, I can feel the warmth in me growing and I never knew that my life would change the day you walked up to me.

As time passes I can see that my outlook on life has changed and I have no one to thank but you.

You have shown me the beauty in these streets that I once saw as dark and gloomy.

You have brought lightness to my soul that I could never in my life thank you for. I smile everyday knowing I get to wake up next to an intelligent beautiful angel whose soul has intertwined with mine.

As I look at you, I know I will never let you slip from my arms as I vow to always bring a smile upon your face.

As I laid my eyes upon you watching you walk down the aisle to me to make our vows to forever to hold. I thank the lord for the beauty he has blessed upon my life.

Once you meet my side and as we make eye contact, I can see my life play out within your eyes and I know my heart and soul are in the perfect hands. As we start are forever with two simple words I DO.

Walking through this world seeing all these wicked things creating all these wicked dreams.

As I lay at night frightened about what wicked things the night brings.

Leaving a dim light on to chase away these wicked things.

Not knowing that once I sleep these wicked things sleep right next to me.

Corrupting my dreams to terrifying nightmares. As I toss and turn trying to escape these wicked things.

Jumping from my sleep with my eyes wide open going back to being terrified of what the night brings.

Gone like the smile that brightened my day.

Gone like the laughter that filled me joy.

Gone like the touch that left me with warmth.

Gone like the hugs that left me secure.

Gone like the voice that left my heart beating.

Gone like the kiss that filled me with passion.

Gone from that day you took your last breath.

Gone from my life until the day we meet again.

You're not gone from the memories that stay with me until my last breath.

As I lay these roses upon your stone I will leave you with these last words

I will carry your memory with me forever in my heart as I wait for the day to hold you in my arms as we tell each other stories of the lives we have seen.

We started our journey on this earth so innocent and full of life as if we knew we could take on the world.

But as the years passed we have been broken down to conform to what others have become as they trapped our free spirits in a cage being held against us.

As we are told what we can and cannot do.

Walking in a line to afraid to walk off the path in fear of the repercussions.

As we hold our tongues in fear of being looked down upon.

We walk as if we live our lives in a factory going down a conveyor belt as they strip us of our personalities.

We have lived our lives to the image they have bestowed upon us without missing a beat, as we daydream of the day we are set free to be who we truly are.

As we sit back and take on the verbal abuse as we plot in our minds the ways we can rebel when the day comes.

On that day we will use our voices and scream out as our free spirits will break free from the cages they have been locked away in.

As we vow to never lose our true selves to sacrifice who

we are for others. Our personalities are what make us beautiful in this world full of diversity.

Your imperfections are beautiful.

Your scars are beautiful.

Your birthmarks are beautiful.

Your skin color is beautiful.

Your mind is beautiful.

Who you are is absolutely beautiful to me, even if I don't know you.

You Are Beautiful.

Through light there is dark
Through dark there is light.

With every smile lies a frown
With every frown lies a smile.

We laugh even though we hide our pain
We seem sad even though we hide our happiness.

Afraid to slip from the faces we show in fear to face what lies below.

Hidden behind the walls we create to keep us safe, not knowing when the pain or fear will fade.

Behind these walls, we cower in fear not knowing how to handle these feelings you show oh so dear.

Two Faced

Two faced like a flip of a coin; let's see what side it lands on.

For whatever side it shows will be the face that I show.

You might get the sweet and nice face or you might just get the conniving mischief face.

The future me that you will see is destined by this coin you see in my hands, so let's take this time to press your luck to see which of me you will see.

You came to me through the darkness of this room as you secretly watched my frustrations grow.

As you made yourself known by wearing a mask, you spoke to me with such enticing words that had me hypnotized by the picture you painted of the future you could give me.

You spoke of the fame you could bring and the talent you can bestow upon me that would eliminate all frustrations.

As you look down upon me you say all
of this can be yours by signing on the dotted line.

Now who would have known by signing this dotted line that my life would be turned upside down by taken to the top of the music world filled with fame, money, love, and cars.

I spend every day living the dream that I have always wanted by playing in front of thousands of people in sold-out arenas hearing them sing the songs I have written. As they scream my name from city to city.

Living this dream that has been granted to me not knowing that the man I signed this contract with is holding my life's string as time runs down by every tick tock of the clock.

With my life's string getting shorter and shorter you have given me a sickness that one cannot come back from. While I sit in the hospital bed with fans sitting outside wishing for me to regain my health.

You visit me one last time without your mask as I look up to see the man I signed this contract with was truly not a man but the devil himself.

As you look down upon me and laugh knowing that you have tricked me into giving you my soul with your enticing words.

You ask me if I have any last words before you truly end my life's string, as I join the club of those who sold their souls before me is "Never knew that the deal I made would end like this

"Through darkness there is light"

You see even with the darkness of night, there is always a light that shines bright.

Breaking its way through the thickness of the night to guide you through these dark times.

If you feel the darkness closing in and dragging you down.

Do not panic or show fear for the light will shine through and wipe away your tears.

Forgive me father for I have sinned, but you see this world is not what it seems for it is filled with sin.

For each day that passes the light is dying out and the saints are starting to fall to sin.

With every sin we commit we still wish to feed the saint within us.

For there is no true saint in this world just those who fall to both.

I can see that you are fading away with each passing day. The life that is held within your eyes is slowly starting to fade.

As I hold your hand the tears start to fall as I pray to god to let you live. I plead with him, telling him that we still have a life to fulfill.

As each day passes we replay the memories of the adventures we have captured. As I watch these memories I can't help the tears that fall as I wish we could go back to when you were full of life.

I tell you of the life we will live once this passes and how we will grow old together as we share our life's story with our grandkids.

You smile my way and tell me you love me. You make me promise that no matter what happens that I will continue to live my life and love again. I look at you and tell you that you will make it out this and that we will live our life together.

As the tears fall you ask me to hold you through the night, as we share a kiss and say I love you as we fall asleep in each other's arms.

I wish I would have known that would have been the last time I hear those words, for I would have held you tighter.

I loved you with everything in me. I gave you my heart and soul as I let you in. Our love grew as we shared our hearts and our dreams to build a life as one.

With every day we grow more in love with each other as we shared experiences and traveled this world.

Together we saw this worlds amazing natural phenomenon and experienced many different cultures everywhere we went.

As time passed I felt you pulling away and becoming distant. Every time I asked what was wrong you would snap at me telling me everything is fine.

Our days that were full of love turned to nightly fights. I would tell you I love you and you would walk away. I can feel us falling apart as I cried for our love to be the same.

I came home to find all your stuff gone and all you left behind was a note. In this note, you stated how sorry you were and how your love for me has faded.

I fell to my knees at your last words as I felt my heart shatter into a million pieces as I cried for it to not be true.

For days I have cried and felt empty as I look around this home we shared, as I see all the memories we made and the love we have created.

I still wake up wishing that it wasn't true, that I will find you downstairs with a smile as you tell me you love me.

Today is the day that I move out of the home we shared for it is just an empty shell of a reminder of what we had.

My heart is slowly healing but is still learning to not yearn for your touch.

I will cherish what we had but I know I need to move on and let you go for me to truly heal.

Your beauty is not defined by others; it's defined by you.

Fire & Ice

As your fingertips glide across my skin setting ablaze upon me as I succumb to the intense passion of who you are.

I lay my hand upon you as I slide it across your chest as the coolness of my skin creates a reaction across the warmth of yours as our bodies intertwined mixing fire and ice together as one.

We look upon each other with a lust that no longer can be held back as our lips meet with the intense passion that we hold for one another.

As our bodies become one we know that our passion will never fade for you are the fire that sets my skin a blaze, as I am the ice that sends coolness to yours.

Life is like a game of chess.

You go through it sacrificing your pawns in your early years for relationships that don't last.

As time passes, and you grow wiser your stronger pieces step forward to protect your heart from those unworthy of such love.

Waiting for the day that a king or queen worthy of your love will step forward to be by your side as you face this world head on hand in hand.

I beg you to lay your gun down.

I know this life is hard and unbearable right now, but if
you pull that trigger your story will be over.

The people in your life will only be able to read the pages in your story
that have lead up to this point, but if you pull that trigger the pages in
your story will be filled with other people's words of who you used to be.

If you pull that trigger you will never know what your future chap-
ters in your story hold.

If you pull that trigger the love and adventure you could hold will
be nothing but the gun powder left behind.

If you pull that trigger you will never know the ways that your life
could be enlightened with the future love you haven't met yet.

So, I beg you please lay your gun down.

I know it's hard right now for I have been in your shoes, but I prom-
ise your story will get better.

Lay your gun down and fight to write your story with your
own words.

Let your strength pour onto these blank pages and fight through
this low point for your story is beautiful and is waiting to be written.

Walking down these streets that are now filled with nothing, but burning, and shattered buildings being haunted by the memories of laughter.

This community used to be filled with people and culture that now have been burned to the ground as the ashes turn the sky grey.

To know that there are only a few of us left to carry out our culture all because of greed, envy, and the pursuit of power.

Walking under the moonlight surrounded by Mother Nature contemplating how I feel so alone in this world.

Talking out loud as I vent out my frustrations to trees around me, as I hear this voice coming from afar.

I look around to see who is there but no one is in sight. Then I hear, "I'm Mother Nature child and I have been hearing everything that you have been saying to my trees"

"I just want to let you know that you are not alone for you have the sun, the moon, and I with you every step that you take"

I ask Mother Nature "how can that be"

She replies "my child the sun kisses your skin every morning with warmth that fills you from within."

"The moon shines upon your skin every night as it helps relax your mind"

"For myself, I am with you wherever you go. You feel me in the wind, the rain, the snow, the trees, the grass, and the dirt that's around you"

"For you see my child, we will be one with you till the end of time"

Walking in the light of love and positivity will always triumph over hate and negativity.

Prayer before death

Now I lay me down to sleep. I pray the lord my soul to keep.

For I shall die before the sun wakes.

I pray that god protects my soul from the vultures lurking through the night.

I know this path to you is filled with such light to bare the coldness of such a night.

With the sins I have committed I pray to you father to forgive me for being naive in my ways.

I know I was lost for some time but I was found in the glory of your light and love.

I have worked hard to live my life walking on the path of love that you have laid out for your children.

For this night is my last and I shall take my last breath with a smile on my face knowing that I will soon get to meet you.

Amen

Do you know your enemy?

Some would say they know the names of their enemies, but would never say the name of their greatest enemy.

Which would be the one that stares back at them in the mirror.

The biggest enemy you have is yourself. The doubts and fears that linger within your own mind are what hold you captive through these times.

As I walk through this valley
I fear no evil for I am the shadow that brings death upon you.

When you visit my valley
do not fear for you may travel safely if it's not our time to meet.

As you walk stay upon the path do not stray away for you may
get lost in the darkness forever to stay.

Death

When you breathe in your first breath death stands beside you.
As you go through your life death walks by your side like a friend
you cannot see.

Death sees your life and patiently waits for your time.

As you reach the ending of your life death sits beside you and lays
their hand upon you letting you finally see them as they look upon
you with a warm smile as they let you know it's time for your soul
to move onward from the physical plane you have walked upon.

Death will lead you to your light walking by your side every step of
the way creating conversation as you talk about the life you lived
for they have seen it.

When death brings you to your light they smile and hug you like a
friend who is saying goodbye.

Death does not frown nor weeps as you leave for they know you
are leaving behind your sufferings to rejoice with those who have
left before you.

Before you cross over they wish you the best in the afterlife, as they
walk back to start the cycle again with someone new.

Remember me on the days you have forgotten.

Remember me on the days that are hard.

Remember me even though my time has come to say goodbye.

Remember me for I shall always remember you.

Remember me for I shall always come back on the day of Dia De Los Muertos for I shall bring our family with me.

Remember me for I shall wait for the day I can hold you in my arms.

Remember me for every tune of the guitar you hear for I shall be by your side.

Remember me for I shall always hold you up even though I am not there.

Remember me for I shall always love you with everything in me.

Remember me for I wait to hear your stories of the life you lived.

Remember me for the day you have forgotten will be the day I fade away.

Remember me for if you pass along our story together I will live within our family for generations to come.

Remember me for I shall live through your memories.

Remember me for I wait by the gates with our family to show you around your new home.

Just never forget to Remember Me.

Dark Skies

The day starts out so bright, as the sun kisses its creations to give them more life.

She whispers in the ears of those who walk on her planet to wake them up for their day. She brings them light and hugs them with such warmth.

Through the day she smiles down as she watches from above.
The hours pass as the day starts to weigh heavy with all that she has seen.

Her mood starts to change as the dark clouds come rolling in bringing darkness across her lands.

Her anger shows through the rumbling of thunder and lightning. As it slowly turns to tears that soak her world.

She weeps for all that she has seen as she leaves to let her great love take over the night for she needs to escape to the other side of her world.

When you think about the life your living do you notice if you are really living your life or just constricting yourself to your daily routine like a ball and chain strapped to your ankle.

Do you ever take the time to just look at the world around you to watch the sunrise to watching the sunset to make way for the moon to shine at night with the stars surrounding the sky like nature's diamonds.

To have the experience of getting lost in the moment to let go of everything in your life in that exact moment for peace and clarity to re-energize your soul from all the chaos in your life.

We need to make memories and experience this world around us every day, because you only have this one life to experience it.

This love started out so beautiful and full of life.

We would steal kisses and speak nothing but love for each other as we lived our lives together.

Years have passed and the words of love you used to speak to me have turned to words of hate.

The hands that held me with such love have turned against me with such rage.

The person I used to love is no longer the same person I once knew, but has turned into this monster that I wonder if this monster was always you.

This home that once held nothing but love and passion now holds nothing but fear and damage.

These bruises left behind in a fit of rage have begun to heal and I know that I can no longer hide what you have created.

When you return I will no longer be here for you to take your rage out on for I know I am worth more than that.

My life will move on and I will forget all of what we once had for the love I have found has finally shown me what true love holds.

Demons plague our world every day from within us, but these demons do not last.

These demons whisper, asking how can anyone love you when you don't even know what love is. You grew up in domestic violence and that's all you will know.
But these demons do not last.

These demons tell you that no one will care if you're gone, and if you were, they won't even miss you. You're nothing but a burden. Kill yourself you're useless. But in the end, these demons do not last.

These demons tell you to go get another fix. You need it and your nothing without it. But these demons do not last.

These demons tell you that you will go nowhere and that you will be nothing in this world. But these demons do not last.

So you see in the end, you are stronger than these demons, and you can overcome what they say to you because, in the end, you are worth something.

You can be loved and love in return. People do love you and will miss you, you are better than that fix, and you can become anything you want when you put your mind to it.

For your demons do not last.

Dear Reader,

Thank you for joining me on this journey and for reading the pages that hold a piece of my soul, my heart, and my mind. I hope that the words within this book have helped you, and have entertained you. I am forever grateful that you have chosen to pick up this book and read the pages within it.

Sincerely,
Melissa Rodriguez